Opuestos:
Abierto y cerrado

Opposites:
Open and Closed

Luana K. Mitten

Rourke
Publishing LLC
Vero Beach, Florida 32964

www.rourkepublishing.com

PHOTO CREDITS: © Matthew Cole: page 3 left; © Marc Dietrich: page 3 right; © Ekaterina Monakhova: page 4, 5, 23, 24; © iofoto: page 7, 8; © William Casey: page 9; © Scott Dunlap: page 11; © Renata Osinska: page 12; © Constant: page 13; © Paul B. Moore: page 15; © Darja Vorontsova: page 16; © JP: page 17; © Jacek Chabraszewski: page 19; © Oddech: page 23

Editor: Kelli Hicks

Cover design by Nicola Stratford, bdpublishing.com

Interior Design by Heather Botto

Spanish Editorial Services by Cambridge BrickHouse, Inc.   www.cambridgebh.com

Library of Congress Cataloging-in-Publication Data

Mitten, Luana K.
  Opposites : open and closed / Luana K. Mitten.
      p. cm. -- (Concepts)
  Learning the concept of opposites through riddles and poetry.
  ISBN 978-1-60472-420-2 (hardcover)
  ISBN 978-1-60472-816-3 (softcover)
  ISBN 978-1-60472-502-5 (hardcover bilingual)
  ISBN 978-1-60472-820-0 (softcover bilingual)
  1. English language--Synonyms and antonyms--Juvenile literature. I. Title.
  PE1591.M646 2008
  423'.1--dc22
                          2008018800

Printed in the USA
CG/CG

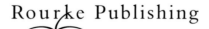

Rourke Publishing

www.rourkepublishing.com – rourke@rourkepublishing.com
Post Office Box 3328, Vero Beach, FL 32964

Abierto y cerrado, abierto y cerrado, ¿cuál es la diferencia entre abierto y cerrado?

Open and closed, open and closed, what's the difference between open and closed?

Cuando duermes, ¡tus ojos están cerrados!

When you sleep, your eyes are closed!

Cuando despiertas, ¡tus ojos están abiertos!

When you wake up, your eyes are open!

Cuando comes, abres y cierras tu boca.

When you eat, you open and close your mouth.

Cuando masticas, ¡tu boca está cerrada!

When you chew, your mouth is closed!

8

Cuando sonríes, ¡tu boca está abierta!

When you smile, your mouth is open!

9

Cuando saludas, abres y cierras tu mano.

When you wave, you open and close your hand.

Cuando pintas, ¡tu mano está cerrada!

When you paint, your hand is closed!

Cuando te lavas, ¡tus manos están abiertas!

When you wash, your hands are open!

13

Cuando agarras una pelota, abres y cierras tus brazos y tus manos.

When you catch a ball, you open and close your arms and your hands.

15

Cuando das un abrazo, ¡tus brazos están cerrados!

When you give a hug, your arms are closed!

16

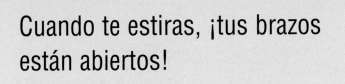

Cuando te estiras, ¡tus brazos
están abiertos!

When you stretch, your arms are open!

17

Cuando corres, abres y cierras tus piernas.

When you run, you open and close your legs.

Cuando te paras, ¡tus piernas están cerradas!

When you stand, your legs are closed!

20

Cuando pateas, ¡tus piernas están abiertas!

When you kick, your legs are open!

Abierto y cerrado, abierto y cerrado, ahora sabes la diferencia entre abierto y cerrado.

Open and closed, open and closed, now you know the difference between open and closed.

Abierto / Open

Cerrado / Closed

Índice / Index

Lecturas adicionales / Further Reading

Child, Lauren. *Charlie and Lola's Opposites.* 2007.

Ford, Bernette. Sorrentino, Christiano. *A Big Dog: An Opposites Book,* 2008.

Falk, Laine. *Let's Talk About Opposites: Morning to Night,* 2007.

Holland, Gina. *Soft and Hard (I Know My Opposites),* 2007.

Sitios web recomendados / Recommended Websites

www.abcteach.com/grammar/online/opposites1.htm
www.resources.kaboose.com/games/read1html
www.learn4good.com/kids/preschool_english_spanish_language_books.htm

Sobre la autora / About the Author

Luana Mitten vive en Tampa, Florida con su familia y su perro, Tuesday. Mientras Luana escribe en su computadora, ¡Tuesday se acuesta en el piso a su lado, con los ojos cerrados!

Luana Mitten lives in Tampa, Florida with her family and their dog, Tuesday. While Luana writes at her computer, Tuesday lays on the floor beside her with her eyes closed!